Extreme
Skydiving

Rob Waring, *Series Editor*

NATIONAL GEOGRAPHIC
LEARNING

Australia · Brazil · Mexico · Singapore · United Kingdom · United States

Words to Know

This story is set in the United Kingdom, in the northern part of England. One of the people in the story comes from Liechtenstein [lɪktənʃtaɪn, -staɪn], a small country in Europe.

 Skydiving. Read the paragraph. Then match each word or phrase with the correct definition.

In the thrilling sport of skydiving, participants can reach velocities of up to 120 miles per hour. First, skydivers jump from airplanes and free fall for thousands of feet as they are pulled to Earth by gravity. Then, they open their parachutes and float into the drop zone to land. In order to go faster, some divers experiment with different techniques to reduce the effects of air resistance, which often slows them down.

1. velocity _____

2. free fall _____

3. gravity _____

4. parachute _____

5. drop zone _____

6. air resistance _____

a. the natural Earth force that pulls objects to the ground

b. a clear space on the ground where skydivers land

c. a large, lightweight sheet attached to a falling person or thing

d. make a rapid downward movement

e. speed as measured in miles per hour or feet per second

f. the force that works against the movement of an object through air

1 mile per hour = 1.61 kilometers per hour

B **The Right Equipment**. Read the definitions. Then label the picture with the correct words or phrases.

A <u>helmet</u> is a safety covering for the head.
A <u>harness</u> is a piece of equipment that secures the parachute to the diver.
A <u>peregrine falcon</u> is one of the fastest animals on Earth.
A <u>rubber suit</u> is a tight piece of clothing used for warmth and reduced air resistance.
The <u>wings</u> of some birds draw back when they're ready to free fall during a hunt.

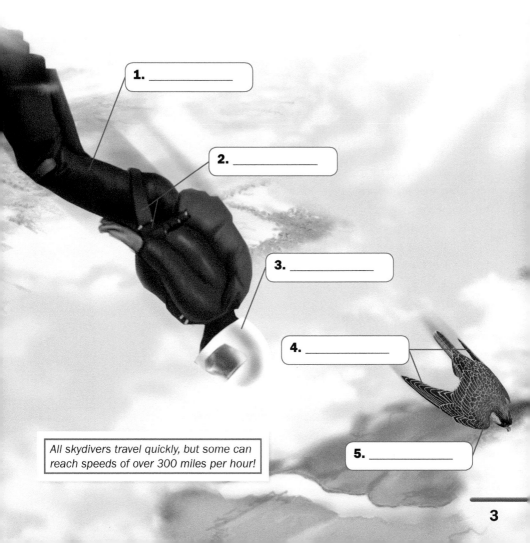

1. _____

2. _____

3. _____

4. _____

All skydivers travel quickly, but some can reach speeds of over 300 miles per hour!

5. _____

Extreme speed is a fundamental part of the sport of skydiving. The average skydiver jumps out of a plane from a height of thousands of feet and free falls. In a free fall, the diver **accelerates**[1] extremely quickly and can reach speeds exceeding 100 miles per hour in a few moments. But following the initial drop, the diver reaches a constant speed of about 120 miles per hour, sometimes known as 'terminal velocity.'

Terminal velocity occurs during a free fall when a person's falling body experiences zero acceleration. To put it simply, the diver's falling body cannot go any faster because he or she has reached a point at which air speed has become **stable**.[2] This inability to increase speed is caused by air resistance, or 'drag,' which slows the body down by creating an opposing force to gravity.

However, not all skydivers are 'average skydivers.' Some are what people call 'speed skydivers.' Speed skydiving is all about finding ways to go beyond terminal velocity and reaching higher and higher speeds. In this highly competitive sport, participants sometimes use scientific approaches—and a lot of imagination—to find ways to fall faster. Mark Calland is one of these competitors, and he is a man who wants one thing: to go faster.

---

[1] **accelerate:** speed up, move faster
[2] **stable:** fixed and unchanging

 CD 2, Track 05

Predict

Which methods of reaching higher speeds
do you think will be mentioned in the reader?
Tell your ideas to a partner or write them in
a notebook. Then read and find out.

Mark is a world-class speed skydiver from England. He describes what it's like to experience the thrill of speed skydiving and reach such extreme velocities. "It's the **adrenaline**[3] rush," he says. "You know that you're going faster than most cars." To this he adds with a smile, "The only thing that's faster than me is possibly a jet engine." Mark goes on to explain that going faster than the world's fastest sports cars is pretty exciting. "You talk to people and they **brag**[4] about their Ferraris and stuff like that," he says. "[In response] you [can] just turn around and say, 'Well, sorry. I go faster than that and I haven't even got an engine on me.'"

Speed skydiving is sometimes referred to as the fastest sport in the world without an engine. The goal of the sport is simple. "Just [to] get out of the plane and try and go as fast as we possibly can in free fall," Mark explains. As one watches diver after diver jump out of a plane and race through the air, the sport looks very easy; however, looks can be very misleading.

---

[3] **adrenaline:** a natural substance produced by the body in times of danger or anger that makes one ready to fight or run away
[4] **brag:** praise one's own successes

Because of air resistance and the resulting terminal velocity, going faster while skydiving is more difficult than it appears—at least for human beings. No matter what height a person jumps from, a normal skydiver in free fall won't go much faster than 120 miles per hour. And once terminal velocity is reached, whether the person falls one minute or one hour, or whether he or she falls 100 feet or one mile—the person will remain at a constant speed of around 120 miles per hour.

While the average person does have a terminal velocity of 120 miles per hour, there are factors that can affect the speed of a diver's fall rather significantly. How one falls and the position of one's body when falling are very important if the goal is to go really fast. These two aspects, as well as weight, influence the effects of air resistance on any object that is falling through the air.

While an average-sized human may have problems beating terminal velocity, there is one creature in nature that has learned how to reach higher speeds: the peregrine falcon. As the bird flies through the air, it's obvious that it's fast; but then it goes into hunting form. It moves its wings back into dive position, points its nose to the earth, and suddenly begins dropping rapidly towards the ground. When it's speeding towards the earth, it's easy to understand why the peregrine is also known as nature's '**guided missile**.'[5] In fact, a peregrine falcon in an attack dive is the fastest animal in the world.

---

[5]**guided missile:** a piece of equipment used in war which flies at extremely high speeds

For some time, nobody knew just how fast the peregrine falcon was, until a man named Ken Franklin decided to find out. Ken conducted an experiment in which he went skydiving with his pet hunting falcon. He took his peregrine in an airplane up to 15,000 feet, after which he released the bird, and then jumped out of the plane himself. When Ken reached terminal velocity, he dropped a **lure**[6] that was made of meat. He hoped that the bird would try to attack and catch the lure, which would allow him to measure the bird's speed. The lure was weighted, or made heavier, to make it fall faster than the bird or him. As expected, the falcon went into an attack dive when the meat was released, as if it were pursuing its **prey**.[7] Both the bird and the meat lure flew through the air at incredibly high speeds, and the bird chased down the lure and caught the meat.

A tiny computer attached to the falcon recorded its speed during the experiment. Surprisingly enough, during its fastest dive, the bird managed to reach an amazing 242 miles per hour! By diving head first and moving its wings back and closer to its body, the peregrine falcon is able to reduce its air resistance and increase its dive speed. Now, the question is: can the falcon's methods be adjusted and used to increase the diving speeds of skydivers?

---

[6]**lure:** something used to attract and catch animals
[7]**prey:** animals killed for food by other animals

Scan for Information

Scan page 13 to find the information.

1. Where is the world speed skydiving championship being held?

2. Who held the British speed skydiving record before the competition?

3. Who is Mark's main competition?

Before a competition, all participants must carefully examine their equipment.

Back among humans, Mark Calland is hoping that a method similar to that of the falcon will help him to better break the limits of terminal velocity. Mark has come to the world speed skydiving championship competition which is being held at a drop zone in the north of England. He's one of the fastest skydivers in the world and the holder of the British record. Today Mark aims to win, but it isn't going to be easy for him. His main competition is going to come from **Marco Wiederkehr**,[8] the national champion of Liechtenstein. Marco is an excellent speed skydiver and a worthy challenger for Mark.

The competitors prepare themselves for their free fall. They put on their uniforms of rubber suits, helmets, and other safety equipment and walk out to the airplane. As they go, they carefully examine their equipment and their **speedometers**[9] to be sure everything is in perfect working order. Once everything has been checked, the participants give a 'thumbs up' sign to indicate that they're ready to go and head to the waiting airplane. As he walks towards the door to join the competitors, Marco turns and says with a laugh, "Well, let's go fast!"

---

[8]**Marco Wiederkehr:** [mɑrkoʊ vɪdərkɛər]
[9]**speedometer:** an instrument that measures the speed of something

As the competition begins, each skydiver performs a series of jumps in order to get the fastest time possible. The techniques used by the competitors vary, but the secret to success in this unusual sport seems to be relatively uncomplicated. All one must do is jump out of an airplane, dive at inhuman speeds toward the ground —sometimes head first—and remain completely relaxed!

Mark explains that for him, a lot of the competition is psychological; it's all about controlling the mind and feelings. He does this by creating a mental picture of what he wants to happen. He describes the process using his own words: "Yeah, you [have got to have] totally … just nothing in your mind at all. You just [have got to] really feel. You've got to feel how your body is flying and how it's reacting." It appears that, like most sports, speed skydiving is about controlling the mind in order to use the body more effectively.

Mark starts preparing for his first jump while he's on the ground. He does so by lying back, closing his eyes, relaxing, and imagining the jump. When he finally gets up in the air, he's ready. He stands near the large door of the plane and steps out into space. As he does so, he slowly moves his head backward and adjusts his body. At last he begins to fall through the air at high speed head first. By going head first—just like the peregrine falcon—the effects of air resistance on his body are reduced and he can go faster.

Mark seems completely relaxed as he flies through the air during the first phase of his jump—the free fall. Then, after reaching his maximum speed, Mark releases his parachute and floats gently to earth. He then lands easily in the drop zone and gathers up his parachute. Amazingly, after falling through the air at an extreme speed and doing something potentially very dangerous, Mark is not even breathing hard. As he calmly walks back to the jump site, he comments on his performance. "**Reasonably**[10] fast for my first jump," he notes and continues to the jump site to get the official reading of his dive speed.

In the competition, the participants use the average speed of their three best jumps. The divers' speeds are measured by speedometers that are located in two tiny computers attached to their harnesses. Back at the jump site, the officials are checking Mark's speed on their computers. His first jump was 302 miles per hour. That's pretty fast, but now it's Marco's turn—and a competitor's standing in a sport like this can change extremely quickly.

---

[10]**reasonable:** acceptable or understandable; as good as expected

Marco is already up in the plane and waiting at the door ready to jump. Now is his big chance to take the lead in the competition. He throws himself from the plane, knowing that he must beat Mark's first dive speed of 302 miles per hour. After about ten seconds, Marco reaches 100 miles per hour, and by 16 seconds, he hits 200! Twelve seconds later, Marco's done it! He's reached a new world record—312 miles per hour, which is 502 kilometers* per hour! Either way it's measured, it means the same thing: Marco's jump was significantly faster than Mark's.

"Marco's got 502," repeats Mark upon hearing the results. It's now clear to him that he has some real competition, but Mark is confident that Marco cannot maintain that extremely high speed on every jump. The winner has to have the fastest average speed over three jumps, and Mark is focusing on going fast **consistently**[11] rather than going fast on just one jump. Besides, Mark has got something special that may allow him to go faster.

---

[11]**consistent:** repeated in the same way or manner
*See page 32 for a metric conversion chart.

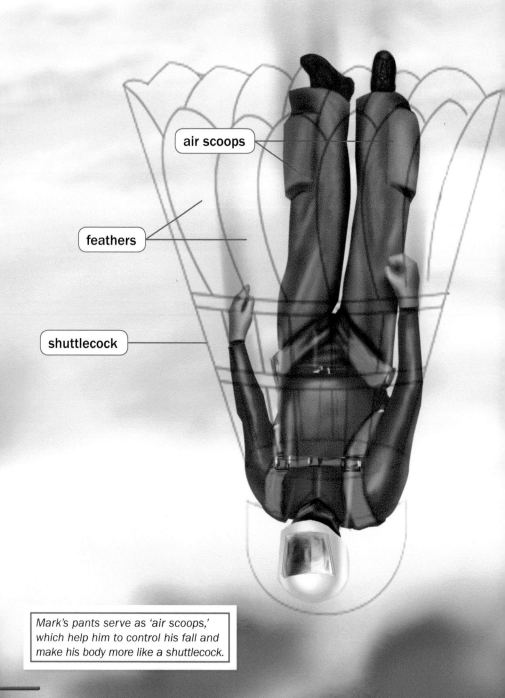

air scoops

feathers

shuttlecock

Mark's pants serve as 'air scoops,'
which help him to control his fall and
make his body more like a shuttlecock.

Speed skydivers must use everything they can to improve the way that they fall through the air in order to go faster than terminal velocity. Taking a scientific approach, they often use specially designed helmets and other types of clothing to help them maintain the best falling position. By using a wind tunnel to test the wind resistance of his body falling through space, Mark has developed a special suit. Interestingly enough, the suit includes a pair of pants that fill with air.

Mark is hoping that the unique air pants he has designed will give him a great advantage. He hopes that they will allow him to better control his fall. The pants are designed to catch the air and allow Mark to better control his movements. By doing so, Mark should be able to maintain the best angle of approach and reach the highest speeds. When using the pants, Mark's body is almost like a **shuttlecock**[12] in a game called 'badminton.' "These pants are big air **scoops**,"[13] he explains. " The bottom half of the pants actually **inflate**[14] and it gives you the shuttlecock effect." As Mark falls through the air, his strongly built upper body is like the rubber tip of a shuttlecock. His air-filled pants act like the feathers at the other end of the shuttlecock.

---

[12]**shuttlecock:** a small object with feathers that is used like a ball in the game of badminton
[13]**scoop:** a deep spoon used to hold an amount of something
[14]**inflate:** fill with air

Mark's aim is to fall through the air just like a shuttlecock does. The pants increase Mark's drag, but they give him much more control. Wearing them makes it easier for him to remain relaxed while he's hanging upside down and flying towards the earth. Gravity does the rest. The more relaxed Mark can be, the faster he falls.

It's time for Mark's next jump. As he begins his free fall through the air, Mark starts with his head down and arms and legs slightly spread out. Then, he pulls his arms close to his body, and pulls his ankles closer together. This form inhibits wind resistance and makes his body more like a shuttlecock. Mark also focuses on keeping his head down and in the correct position since it will enable him to go faster. He's able to show great control and has a good jump, but no one is sure if his new air-filled pants will bring him a win in the competition.

It's now Marco's turn to jump again. He doesn't have inflatable pants like Mark, just a smooth rubber suit which is tight-fitting to keep air resistance at a minimum. As the airplane climbs higher and higher into the sky on its way to the jump point, Marco sits quietly in his seat with his eyes closed. It seems that it's not only Mark who uses his mind to help control his body. Finally, Marco stands to get ready for the jump. As the light at the front of the jump area of the plane turns green, Marco goes to the door and dives into the air. After a few moments, he moves his body forward so he's falling head first. Once he initiates this move, Marco begins diving at incredible speeds towards the earth until at last, he disappears from view.

Unfortunately after his very fast first dive, Marco is unable to keep up the record-high speeds. This jump is a disappointment and he's unable to control his fall. As he works to keep himself pointed straight down during the jump, he goes through some clouds and **wobbles**.[15] As he does so, he loses valuable miles per hour. Once he reaches the ground, Mark checks in about the jump as he picks up his parachute. "Marco, how was your jump?" asks Mark as Marco gathers his own parachute. "[I] got into the clouds, then [it was] a bit wobbly," Marco replies. "[My] speed is not so high [as] the maximum speed," he adds as he checks the tiny computer on his wrist.

---

[15]**wobble:** move in an unbalanced way from one side to another

On his next and final jump, Mark, however, doesn't wobble. He flies like the wind as he jumps from the plane. The skydive goes beautifully and Mark is able to maintain control throughout it. His specially-designed pants are really working! The wind-filled clothing gives him the advantage he needs to achieve three very good jumps and his average speed is the highest of all the competitors.

The world speed skydiving competition has come to an end and the huge silver **trophies**[16] are set on a large table for everyone to see. It's the moment that they all have been waiting for; it's time to announce the winners. As the names for the various event categories are read, they finally come to the one that Mark wants to hear. "Men's Event, first place … Mark Calland," says the judge, and Mark proudly steps forward to collect his first-place trophy. Mark's scientific approach to skydiving has paid off, and for today at least, it's made him the best speed skydiver in the world!

---

[16]**trophy:** a prize, such as a silver cup or bowl

Answer the questions. Then write a report about this story or tell a friend about it. Use information from your answers.

1. Who is Mark Calland and what was his goal in the competition?

2. Who was his main competitor and how did he perform?

3. What is Mark's invention and how does it work?

After You Read

1. Which of the following results in terminal velocity?
   A. a free fall
   B. zero acceleration
   C. air resistance
   D. speeds over 120 miles per hour

2. What opinion does Mark Calland express on page 7?
   A. Car racing is more thrilling than skydiving.
   B. Speed skydivers should compete against airplanes.
   C. Sports car drivers brag too much about their cars.
   D. Reaching high speeds without an engine is impressive.

3. Which of the following affect the speed of a fall?
   A. the height from which a person falls
   B. the distance a person falls
   C. the position of the falling person's body
   D. the length of time a person falls

4. In paragraph 2 on page 10, to what does 'it' in 'its dive speed' refer?
   A. a lure
   B. a bird
   C. a computer
   D. an experiment

5. What does Marco's comment on page 13 probably illustrate about him?
   A. He is not very competitive.
   B. He has a fear of high places.
   C. He has a playful attitude.
   D. He thinks he can beat Mark.

6. What does the word 'inhuman' mean on page 14?
   A. overall
   B. unconscious
   C. cruel
   D. astonishing

7. Which of the following is NOT mentioned as part of the equipment a speed skydiver uses when competing?
   A. glasses
   B. parachute
   C. speedometer
   D. harness

8. The average speed of each competitor is _____ three jumps.
   A. comes from
   B. based on
   C. totaled by
   D. analyzed by

9. An appropriate heading for paragraph 2 on page 21 is:
   A. Diver Designs New Uniforms for All
   B. Feathers and Rubber Decorate Diver's Pants
   C. New Suit Doesn't Inflate as Expected
   D. Theory of Pants Similar to Shuttlecock

10. Mark's new pants help improve his speed by:
    A. creating less air resistance
    B. replacing his parachute
    C. allowing him more control of his body
    D. increasing the strength of the wind

11. What's the main reason why Marco's second jump isn't successful?
    A. He falls through a cloud and becomes unbalanced.
    B. His first jump was too fast.
    C. He goes head first.
    D. He doesn't have inflatable pants.

12. What does the writer probably think about competitive speed skydiving?
    A. Only divers with great equipment will be successful.
    B. Beating others is a result of chance and luck only.
    C. Winning depends on many circumstances.
    D. People from the northern part of England have an advantage.

A HISTORY OF
SKYDIVING

Although there is some evidence that parachutes appeared in China in the 1100s, the earliest recorded example of skydiving is slightly later. Leonardo da Vinci has been attributed with designing the first drafts of a parachute-like mechanism. In about 1495, he designed a six-meter-long* triangular parachute which was held together by flexible wooden sticks. Since airplanes or other methods of flying had not been invented yet, the testing of da Vinci's parachute was limited to jumps from trees, towers and cliffs. In July 2000, British skydiver Adrian Nichols tested da Vinci's design. Nichols stated that, although there were safety issues due to the parachute's weight, the flight was definitely smoother than a modern parachute.

The First Modern Parachute

The first parachute that was similar to those used today was invented by a Frenchman named André-Jacques Garnerin. As a soldier, Garnerin was taken prisoner in Hungary where he began experimenting with parachutes as part of his plan to escape. In 1797, several years after being freed, he constructed the first modern parachute. His design consisted of a rather inflexible framework covered with white cloth and looked a lot like a large umbrella. He made a successful 975-meter jump from a hot-air balloon in 1797, and in 1799 his wife, Jeanne-Genevieve, became the first woman to use a parachute to make a similar jump.

The Birth of Skydiving

Parachuting moved to another level after the invention of the airplane in the early 1900s. During World War I, parachutists became an important part of the fighting forces. This brought attention to parachuting and after the war, parachutists began to appear in public performances. However, it was many years before the term 'skydiving' was created, and skydiving wasn't actually accepted as a sport by the World Air Sports Federation (WASF) until the mid-1950s.

Some of the World's Skydiving Records

Type of Competition	Details	Location	Date
Largest Freefall Formation	400 people	Udon Thani, Thailand	2006
Largest Freefall Formation (Head Down)	69 people	Chicago, Illinois	2007
Largest Canopy Formation	100 people	Lake Wales, Florida	2007
Accuracy	Svitlana Dyachok	Kiev, Ukraine	2004

Skydiving Competitions

As the popularity of the sport grew, the WASF developed rules for competitions and teams and individuals began to compete for prizes in a wide variety of areas, including the following:

- Largest Freefall Formation (the largest group jumping at the same time)

- Largest Freefall Formation Head-Down (the largest group jumping head first at the same time)

- Largest Canopy Formation (the largest group touching each other's open parachutes)

- Accuracy (the competitor who achieves the most accurate repeated landings on a three-centimeter-wide target).

CD 2, Track 06

Word Count: 388

Time: _____

Vocabulary List

accelerate (4)

adrenaline (7)

air resistance (2, 3, 4, 8, 10, 17, 25)

brag (7)

consistent (18)

drop zone (2, 13, 17)

free fall (2, 3, 4, 7, 8, 13, 17, 22)

inflate (21, 25)

gravity (2, 4, 22)

guided missile (8)

harness (3, 17)

helmet (3, 13, 21)

lure (10)

parachute (2, 3, 17, 25)

peregrine falcon (3, 8, 10, 17)

prey (10)

reasonable (17)

rubber suit (3, 13, 25)

scoop (20, 21)

shuttlecock (20, 21, 22)

speedometer (13, 17)

stable (4)

trophy (26)

velocity (2, 4, 7, 8, 10, 13, 21)

wings (3, 8, 10)

wobble (25, 26)

Metric Conversion Chart		
Area		
1 hectare = 2.471 acres		
Length		
1 centimeter = .394 inches		
1 meter = 1.094 yards		
1 kilometer = .621 miles		
Temperature		
0° Celsius = 32° Fahrenheit		
Volume		
1 liter = 1.057 quarts		
Weight		
1 gram = .035 ounces		
1 kilogram = 2.2 pounds		